Take it b

Chloë Jacquet

Black Eyes Publishing UK

Take it by the Line
By Chloë Jacquet

© Chloë Jacquet, 2020

Published by Black Eyes Publishing UK, 2020
Brockworth, Gloucestershire, England
www.blackeyespublishinguk.co.uk

ISBN: 9781913195106

A CIP catalogue record for this title is available from the
British Library.

Cover illustration: Ben Williams

Cover design: Jason Conway, cre8urbrand.
                       www.cre8urbrand.co.uk

For poetry lovers and haters alike

Take it by the Line

Contents

11   Poetry
12   Rattle
13   It's Not You It's Me *
14   P@&try
19   Haiku
20   Dear Mr Colleague *
23   The Post Mistress
24   The Courtroom *
27   Untitled
28   The Breakup
29   Shipwreck
30   Temptation
31   Time
32   Danger
33   The Getaway
34   Hospital
35   Transfusion
36   My Depression Is
38   My Friend
39   Custard
40   I'll Stick With Chocolate
41   Woman Seeking *
42   The Girl and The Ghost
43   There Might Just Be a Storm *
48   The Woman on My Commute
49   The Deer
50   Jars
51   Wolf Moon
52   Toy Gun
55   Eggs
56   Mushroom
59   Skylight
61   Book Review

62   I Met a Boy
64   Why Do We Pray?
65   God's Mum
66   Gun
68   Mouthful
69   Door
70   Idiot Check
73   The Liberation of Women
74   Gropadin™ *
76   What Makes a Man? *
79   Caterpillars
80   Body Con *
83   Big Bang
84   Can Opening
86   Waterboard
87   Outside
88   Why Reading in Public is Cool
89   Words
90   Birthday
91   The Dealer *

95   Biography
97   Acknowledgements

Poems with a star (*) next to the title indicate those for which a video is available on YouTube.

*These can be found by searching for **ChloeJPoetry***

Do check back regularly as more get added.

Poetry

Like the lyrics to a song
only braver
for without the music
you have to face the words.

Rattle

I am a rattle,
a hollowed gourd
filled with bead and seed
shaped emotions.

They roll easily

      too
easily
    inside
        me.

The smallest thing

and I am   moved
    I am   shaken

and it can take overly long

for me to

     settle.

I am a rattle.

Can you hear
     me
       feel?

It's Not You, It's Me

It's not you, it's me.
I know it's a cliché
but what do you want me to say?
It's definitely me.

No, really, it isn't you!
It's not a good time for me right now
I feel I should be alone somehow
so, that's what I'm going to do.

Please try to understand
I just can't share a bed with you
I can't even bring myself to touch you.
It's not something I planned.

Just the thought of you getting turned on
to me, right now, is just so, so wrong.
I want us to take a break.
Perhaps in a couple of months it'll feel like a mistake

and we can get back together
but in this hot weather
I just can't hack it.
Goodbye my sweet, sweet electric blanket.

P@&TRY – A (mostly) True Story

Picture the scene -
a comic book
brought to the silver screen:
a windy, wintry night
black and white rain slashes orange streetlights
in a city
that could pass as Gotham.
Passers-by clutch their coats
sodden trousers clinging to their thighs
scarves wrapped around their throats
as they splash through a cobbled street
like they're walking on water.

Halfway along, in a set-back corner,
is an open door and a single shining light.
We enter.
Up some stairs and to the right
is a restaurant
where a group of Asian holidaymakers
are enjoying dinner.

To the left is a small, wood panelled bar
from which comes the sound
of a voice at a mic.
They're having a spoken word night.

Here we meet our hero.

The small room is packed
so, pint in hand
he stands at the back
by the door
broad shoulders against the wall

stubble and square jaw
all smouldering
and brooding
his eyes on the stage.

We follow his gaze.

The participants take turns
to come and share.
The atmosphere is electric
as one after the other
bares a piece of their soul.
There is love, there is pain,
hope, anger and comedy gold.
There are rhymes, raps
followed by high fives, hugs and claps.

Passers-by get drawn in
by the applause and cheering.
On tiptoes they peer
before squeezing in
to join the audience
grab a drink and listen
caught up
in the joy and validation
of hearing someone else's emotion
opinion
or experience
that they relate to.

Pan back to our hero.

There's a sound on the landing.

Turning, he sees

that the Asian people
having finished their meal
have come over
and are stood at the door.
The room now can't fit any more.
Intrigued, they're watching and filming
the proceedings.

Up the stairs comes a gang of villains
made up of a gentleman
and three younger women:
a kingpin and his skittles.
They're out on the town
they mean to party
they've had a few drinks
they're getting rowdy.

There is a shift in the air
the light bulbs flicker.
The hairs on our hero's neck bristle
instinctively he senses trouble.

As they make their way up
the pack of rebels
spots the sightseers
on the landing.

They stop.

The man slowly lowers his hood
the rainwater from his long black coat
pooling where he is stood.

He begins to tease,
"are you Chinese or Japanese?"

He jeers,
"it's not for your kind here."
The tourists turn in confusion.
His top lip lifts into a joker's sneer
he bounds the last steps
towards one of the men
ramming his face up against his.
"Triads!"
he hisses
whilst his sidekicks
egg him on
with sniggers and eyelashes.

Inside, performers sparkle
spectators marvel
oblivious.

Our hero,
hearing what's being said,
starts to see red.
A small muscle twitches
at the side of his head.
The hulk inside
begins to rise.

Faster than a dart
he uses his smarts.

Drawing on the verbal art,
that quasi martial art,
older than writing itself
going back as far as prehistory
he turns to the gang
smiles and says
"come on in, there's poetry."

Time slows to a standstill.
The clique freezes
as the words and their meaning
hit them like a weapon.

"P@&try?!" – the kingpin spits it like venom.
His face contorts in horror
he's struck by a sudden pallor.
The skittles too recoil in disgust.
It's as though our hero has cussed
with the most offensive word
any of them has ever heard.

"Let's go," one of the women starts to say.
"Yeah, let's get out of here," pleads another
turning ashen grey.
The kingpin pauses, staring with hate
directly into our hero's face

before finally giving a shudder
and walking away
his jaw set
muttering under his breath
"P@&try?! F%ck that sh*t!"

The devils step back out
into the cold and dark of the night
our hero turns back into the light
of the bar.

Shoulders against the wall
once more
he sips his pint quietly
and wonders at the power of poetry.

Haiku

Smoked shed loads of weed,
overthrew the government.
It was a high coup.

Dear Mr Colleague,

I'm so glad we spoke after that meeting,
the one where you went for wholly undermining
both me and everything that we'd agreed to do
and basically, made out all my hard work was done by you.
But that wasn't the worst of it, oh no sirree.

The worst was what you then saw fit to say to me
when I went to confront you after the fact
because of course I have far too much tact
to bring it up in front of everyone.
I waited till after you were done
and there only remained just us two -
thought it'd be the more professional thing to do.

You cut me right off with
"Aww, I think I've upset you,"
with that condescending look, right on cue.
You then asserted it was unfortunate timing -
a few days after my grandmother's passing -
and that therefore I was overreacting.

So, that was the tactic you were going to pursue
pre-emptively discrediting my point of view.

Still, I calmly defended my position
said what I had to say
and you came back with
"I'm sorry you feel that way."

Here's the thing with what you said to me
and I think there's a few here who might well agree
you made the whole issue about my emotions
ignoring the fact that they stemmed from your actions.

Making my feelings the problem in the situation
was a demeaning, patronising attempt at domination.

You put yourself on a pedestal of fact, truth and logic
and tried to reduce me to irrational hysteric
further explained by the fact I was grieving;
how on earth could I possibly be disagreeing?

I wouldn't be surprised if you were secretly wondering
whether maybe, just maybe, I was going to start crying?
Tell me something else, go on, I'm curious
did you think it was my period that was making me
furious?

You refused to consider you might be at fault
so resorted to a pathetic, sexist default.
You seem to consider yourself as a big mighty brain
and me, mere ovaries over which you can reign.
How dare I challenge your God given superiority?
Tell me, are you one of those guys
who likes to grab 'em by the pussy?

There was no evidence of any contrition
could your pride really not handle such an admission?
Or more likely you knew exactly what you were doing.
You just assumed that I'd roll over saying
"Oh Mr. Colleague you are so big and strong
you couldn't possibly do anything wrong."

But, when you realised from the look on my face
that wasn't remotely going to be the case
you deprived me of the right to have an opinion
which, had you even bothered to listen
you'd have found to be based on a good education
years of experience and very sound judgement.

Heaven forbid – I might have come out triumphant.

I'm not saying I'm always right
(although in this case I clearly am)
I'm just saying that if you really were such a big brave man
you wouldn't use base tactics to try to shoot me down
whilst wearing your imaginary penis-shaped crown.

Newsflash for you, if you'll take the time to hear it:
carry on Mr Colleague. I can take all of your shit.
Think you can dominate me? Really, not a chance
'cos since the day I was born I've been dancing this dance
so, I have piles of practice and plenty more energy
and each day I'm going to prove you're not better than me.
In fact, any opportunity I get, I'll do this too -
I'll show your sexist ass that I'm smarter than you.

Yours sincerely,
Your Female Colleague

The Post Mistress

I go through the mail,
steal people's love letters
and pretend they're for me.

The Courtroom

Ladies and gentlemen of the jury
you must find my client, the defendant, "not guilty"
on the counts of grievous bodily harm
and aggravated robbery.

We are about to prove
that it was not the fault of the accused
that she robbed the jewellery shop
and that the owner got shot.

Of course, I do sympathise
that the owner was terrified
when she aimed the gun between his eyes.

Prosecution went into great detail
about how he no longer feels safe
working in retail
that he can't sleep at night
and wakes up in a fright
at the slightest noise,
BUT ladies and gentlemen
he had a choice.

Ask yourselves this, why was he open so late?
Doesn't that feel a bit like bait?
Why would he put himself in that position?
Opposing counsel say he's trying to earn a living
but if you ask me
he might just have known exactly
what he was doing.
I'd go so far as saying
that he was asking for it
and we are only here because now he regrets it.

Case in point, he chose to put all his best
most enticing stock in his window display.
There is no better way to say,
"come and get it,
you know you want it!"
That right there was provocation
a downright, blatant invitation.
It was out there
for all to see.
If he didn't want to be robbed
he should have had more modesty.

I am therefore sure you will agree with me
that proves consent to the robbery.

Furthermore, ladies and gentlemen
it just boils down to oestrogen.
Girls will be girls!
The prosecution claims this was a disturbing act
but it is a fact
that girls are drawn to things that are pretty
such as jewellery
it has nothing to do with greed
but is actually a biological need.
Therefore, to take it is their right
there isn't even a crime here to indict.

Finally, ladies and gentlemen of the jury
it would not be in the interest of justice
to find the defendant guilty.
It would ruin her career prospects
and put an end to her sporting prowess.
She is an accomplished athlete
and a sentence would mean she can no longer compete.

And hasn't she already been punished enough
by being dragged through this ludicrous trial
during which she has been defiled
and which, for her, has been exceedingly tough?
She's been vilified on social media
she can't go out without people shouting at her.
A guilty sentence would be too high a price to pay
for 20 minutes of action anyway.

In summary,
ladies and gentlemen of the jury,
you cannot blame a lady
for wanting to take jewellery
that was put on blatant display late at night
so, you must do what is right.
You must reject this so-called victim's fanciful claims
that he now finds himself at pains
to live a normal life
and that everything is all struggle and strife
as my learned colleague so eloquently argued.

You must be more shrewd:
he wanted it
he was asking for it
it was not my client's fault for taking it
therefore, she MUST BE ACQUITTED.

I rest my case.

Untitled

She stands defiant
a thigh thrust forward
her jaw a horizon
lips a slip apart
head turned and distant gaze
proud nose pointed
bare nipple audacious
slate skin mottled and marked.
Her hair flares behind her
Liberty's flame.

She is only a shape I see
in the bathroom tiles
but when I escape there
holding back tears
she dances for me
and that must mean something.

The Breakup

She slowly slices down the front of his chest
from Adam's apple to navel.
He makes no move
only listens to see whether he'll hear his heart
beat louder through the gaping hole
or whether his other organs might make a sound.
She parts the lips of the wound wide
peeling them back
before breaking open the birdcage of his ribs
spreading the ladders like doors.
She reaches in and catches his panicking heart
pulls it out.
She pauses, stares up at him, waiting
clutching the beating muscle.
He remains motionless and silent.
So she swiftly slices, dices then throws it in the air
like confetti.
She looks at him once more, blinks, then walks away.

He still says nothing.

Shipwreck

I've no captain, no rudder
navigating a wild terrifying ocean
lured by mermen and sirens.
Flung over the crest of waves
thrown into trenches and troughs
broken mast, sails all a-flutter.
No lighthouse for the fog.
Lurching towards jagged cliffs
cold spray on my neck
vomiting over my own prow.
Barnacles and seaweed
pulling me down.
Little nutshell lost
in the never-ending
expanse of water.
Flailing, floundering
disappearing under.

I hope that a thousand years from now
someone will find me and pull me up from the deep
and see that I was filled with gold.

Temptation

Tempted to look back
to revisit history
to feel the familiar
the comfortable, the known
and just to be touched
rather than alone.

But then you let me down
and I remember

why I can't be

around

you.

Time

What kind of magic is this?
Yesterday your five fingers
fitted around the smallest of mine.
Tomorrow those five fingers
will be too few
to count the years since then.

How can the simplest of ingredients
make something grow
so fast.
Can food, water and air
really be all it takes?
Or do you eat time too?

Every grain of sand
from the castles you build
is a minute you thieve
from us
like the tooth fairy
hiding under your pillow
steals your milk teeth.

I'm learning that time
is measured
in teeth
      in sand
            in fingers

I'll keep letting you take mine.

Danger

Your hand opens like an anemone.
Mine fits inside it like prey.

Your breathing sounds like the sea.
I am a lone figure on the biting beach.

You want nothing but good for me
and yet I perceive danger.

The Getaway

A week
a whole week of lovers' holiday:
blue water, pebbles and parasols
wine, cigarettes, baguettes
no telly.

A week
a whole week of daytime swims
sun on our backs, drives to the market
flights of swallows, evening strolls
no telly.

A week
a whole week of you and me
and me and you, of conversations
always facing you, no other soul to talk to
no telly.

A week
a whole week of close-up freeze-frames of you.
Please let it end.
I am fucking sick of your face.

Someone find me a telly.

Hospital

Age 3,
my dad in one hand
a milkshake for my mother
in the other
entering the hospital
to go meet my baby sister.

Age 33,
my dad in one hand
my mother
in the other
entering the same hospital
to learn about her cancer.

Transfusion

In the plasma river
millions, billions of little round boats
red rubber rings, literal life preservers
borrowed from someone else
to keep you alive
for me.

My Depression Is

My depression is an indulgence
sweet, languid and comfortable.
It feels safe because it's
my oldest friend.
It's a bed, a sofa, a room of security
a warm heavy blanket to wrap over
and luxuriate in.
I know it pins me down
but that kind of suits
because action is hard.
My depression is a relief
it's in charge, so I no longer have to be.
Yes, it is dull and painful
but it's familiar and easy.
It saps more strength out of me
than it takes me to step
out of it.
I surrender.
My depression is divine
a fine wine
a drug.
It is chocolate, chocolate, chocolate.
It feeds my soul
with thoughts that it likes me to believe:
I'm worthless, pointless, hopeless
and there is something reassuring in that.
If everything is already dark
there is no risk of losing light.

My depression is safety.
I won't need to climb a ladder
if it has no rungs.
No need to push a door

if I know it's locked.
My depression is convenient
failure is not failure when you expect to fail
it's a triumph.
My depression is a validation.
It says "I told you so."

Don't get me wrong
I adore not being depressed
it's the biggest victory over myself.
But I won't lie
as shameful as it is to admit
a part of me relishes it
when it comes to visit:
my destructive, seductive lover
unhealthy partner
obsessive, clingy and jealous
overbearing and manipulative.
My depression has groomed me successfully.
Succumbing to it is effortless.

When I say I'll slip into something more comfortable
it's into the grey cashmere jumper of my depression
that swaddles me and rocks me like a baby.
So, I'll see you later.
I might be here a while.

My Friend

"Just bring your lovely self," she says.
But I don't want to.

I want to leave my lovely self at home.
I want to bring my bitchiest
grumpiest, rudest self.
I want to abandon the self-censorship
the political correctness
the social norms
the control of my feelings
the biting of my tongue.

And she lets me
which is why she is my friend.

Custard

There are few things
that are more obscene
than a cup of coffee
with no custard cream

I'll Stick with Chocolate

I've never been a size 6
so, I don't know if I'd like it
but I have eaten chocolate
and I do know that I love it.
I'm not much of a risk taker
I don't like gambling.
I'll stick with chocolate

because I'm pretty sure
I love chocolate more
than being a size I've never been before.

Woman Seeking

I like them dark.
Fair is ok too
but not ginger.

I prefer chunky to thin.

Age doesn't bother me as long as they're not past it.

Rich is nice – full on sugar daddy.

They do have to be sweet.
I don't mind a hard exterior
as long as they're soft on the inside.

But not broken
or flaky
can't have them crumbling or falling apart
the second they get themselves into hot water.

I'm pretty voracious
so, it probably won't last long.
Basically, I'm looking for a very, very
short term relationship

with a biscuit.

The Girl and The Ghost

That girl is in love
unrequited, unreciprocated love.
In a relationship with a ghost
a ghost inside her mind.
He, out in the real world
is blissfully unaware
of her eyes on him.
He gives her nothing
no reason, no hope, no sign, no clue.

Yet still, she reads it all
things that aren't there
except in the spirit world
beneath her hair.
Happier in there
she spends more and more time
inside her mind
withdrawing further in
to be with him
till she becomes the ghost
and he becomes the world.

There Might Just Be a Storm

Picture a girl
maybe 19,
she lives the kind of life
girls from other worlds dream.

She's completed school.
Now she's at Uni
learning to be a lawyer.
Fancies George Clooney.

She's independent.
She's confident and free.
Has a lovely boyfriend
he gave her a key.

Her present is carefree
her future is bright.
The only time that she's afraid
is the walk home alone at night.

Now picture another girl
of a similar age.
Same time, same place
but somehow full of rage.

For some reason she's lost
there's nowhere she can belong
so, she goes online
finds a religious song.

She's found a cause to believe in
something for which to fight
not seeing that if it's such a secret
then it just cannot be right.

Whilst girl number 1
goes home for Sunday roasts

girl number 2 withdraws
from those who love her most.

She escapes to a distant land
where she receives training.
She's given to an older man
her mind he's inflaming.

And she looks up to him
and the rest of the dusty clan.
They've given her a purpose
They're hatching up a plan.

Friday

Girl 1 is at a bar
with a group of friends
chatting, laughing, drinking
celebrating the weekend.
Everyone's sitting outside
because it's still so warm.
They talk about the weather.
There might just be a storm.

Girl 2 is in a car
heading into town.
She too is with some friends
but each wears a silent frown.

As girl 1 hugs her boyfriend
amongst music and fairy lights,

girl 2 is rounding the corner
preparing for her night.

It starts with pops and bangs
sounds like firecrackers.
No one really reacts
until someone's blood splatters

across another's face.
Then instantly there's panic.
They all drop to the floor.
The shooting sounds like static.

Suddenly it stops.
Deathly silence.

Girl 1 understands
this is terrorist violence.

As nothing seems to move
she gently lifts her head
all around her people
are dead or playing dead.

She sees girl number 2,

a resolute look on her face.
In her right hand is a trigger
a belt around her waist.

As girl 2 stepped so quietly
no one heard her come.
The living think it's over
those able, stand and start to run.

Girl 2 shouts something out
and presses down her thumb.
Her body is annihilated
and half the scrum succumb.

Girl 1 still on the floor
ears ringing and confused
slowly realises
she is able to move.

She feels no pain at all
she opens both her eyes.
Someone's screaming near her
she hears sirens in the skies.

As rescue comes bursting in
she knows she has survived
but not her lovely boyfriend
he's lying by her side
blood pouring from his chest.
His ribs poke out like spurs.
His watery green eyes
are staring up at hers.

Although girl number 2
failed to take her life
girl number 1 has
lost her way of life.

She's lost her sense of freedom
her entire existence has changed.
Now it's not just walking home alone
that makes her afraid.

We all now know a little of that fear
as we walk our days and nights
but we mustn't stop living free
our forefathers earned us those rights.

Especially as fear is what they're after
fear is what makes them seem so strong.
But look past the shadow of a spider
and you'll see its legs aren't that long.

As we're gathered in this room
to share words, to laugh, to sing
let's show them we're far braver
and we will carry on living.

The Woman on My Commute

She navigates the path along the road
bent over, hunched and bundled against the cold.
A coracle struggling to sail to work
a raft, too small to fight against
relentless rolling waves of wind, like tides
beneath a day too indolent to rise.
Her breath a jellyfish of mist suspended
in churning, swirling, slum-grey seas of fog.

The Deer

Her legs settle at an angle
geometrically impossible.
Her head resting on its side
one eye wide
looking to the sky, and the past
the other eyelid pressed down by the grass.
Her camel coat, intact, immaculate
the fine hairs infinite.
One ear is twitched by the wind
as if caught by the thinned
sound of a god calling.
Her ballerina-pointe hooves, pitch black
which once danced so lightly over leaves
now frozen at the end of the melody
lie in stark contrast to the dull grey asphalt
that witnessed her final halt.
She who was so self-conscious
bashful and anxious
would die of shame to see herself lay
on such crude and public display.

Jars

From floor to ceiling the shelves ladder to hell.
In the dusk's low light, the jars, vials and flasks
glow amber and tarnished gold.
The shapes within throw shadows against the birch boards
tiny tumefied heads, conjoined twins
foetuses without a face.
Beyond the glass
an acrid smell permeates the air
as the innocent hang in their fluid
malformed and desperate.

The room lies still, apart from the scuttling
of spiders seeking flies that the corpses cannot attract
their waxy, flaccid flesh deprived of the right to decay
banished from meeting the worm.
The aborted sing a sonorous incantation of silence.

In the village below, the people lie restless
behind their panes of glass.
As the sun sinks under the windowsills
the moon takes its place
casting a pallid silver glow over the jars.
Night truly begins.

A two-headed figure twitches
and a one-eyed baby blinks.

Wolf Moon

The night is lighter

more feather than tar
as the wolf moon howls its glow.

Gone the heavy woollen mantle
enveloping
the shapes of trees and houses
dulling
their edges
crushing, suffocating
the lives beneath it.

Instead a diaphanous silk shawl floats
above.
There is space between earth
and sky

to stand and not touch it
even with the tips of fingers.

Three owls wing this newfound void
and I am lifted.

Toy Gun

You go back off to Afghan
leaving behind your little man
now old enough to miss you
to feel the void you leave behind.
You're parting from your sweet patient wife
who's unaware of the extent of your strife
although she does have an inkling
but it just doesn't bear thinking.

She doesn't want the little one worrying
so, they carry on with life
waiting for you to come home
from that far distant unknown.
A red cross on the calendar
a ceremony together
after every day
counting down the weeks
till they get to kiss your cheeks
hold you in their arms
and for her to give you her charms.
They remain strong
though time seems long.

You write when you can
Skype when you can
but not too often
it hurts to see your little man's
face on the screen
so eager so keen
knowing he's miles away
and you're running out of things to say
because you can't tell the truth
can't say how viscerally you miss them

scared for your life on every mission
that you're exhausted
afraid, disgusted
by what you have to do
broken physically and mentally too
the thought of them
the only thing that gets you through.
No longer sure why you enlisted
it was exciting the first time you got called up
but you'd no idea how much it'd fuck you up
and now it's catching up with you.
It's taken its toll on you.

You can't admit
the nights you stay up
throwing up
the nightmares, the flashbacks
the panic attacks
stifled sobs in the pitch black.
So you show a smile
just for that short while
you talk of how it's all ok
there's good food every day
you've made good mates
you're all tight
hang out and chill at night
play cards under the moonlight.
Lies, lies, lies
they help you survive.
But
if you said it how it really is
spoke of the fear
the screams, the cries
the fires in the skies
corpses covered in flies

the ripped limbs, the torture
the shots, the mortar
people losing son and daughter
your little boy
might not play with his toys
that look like guns
thinking that war is fun
that he's gonna join up
when he grows up
so he can be just like you and
have fun adventures just like you do.
'Cos you know what he'd go through
that he might end up being one
whose calendar crosses cease to none
before his tour is done.

Can there ever really be such a thing as a toy gun?

Eggs

What if
as a woman is born with all her eggs
we were born with all our days
inside our heads
and our lives were just to watch them unfold
entirely uncontrolled
like a strange, late-night movie
on cable TV?

Mushroom

That thing inside
that loves to hide
is like a mushroom.
It needs the dark to bloom
needs our shame
our pain
that constant internal blame.

"Why can't I be normal
do things that are usual?
What is wrong with me?
Mustn't let anyone see.
They'll think I'm weak
they'll think I'm a freak
mustn't let them hear it in the way I speak
the way I look
the way I move
the way I breathe.

Smile.
It's just for a while
till I get to retreat indoors
between those four walls
and my face can sag.
I can drag
my sorry ass back onto that couch
and slouch
because I am exhausted
at putting on a show
so, they won't know."

Meanwhile, deep down in that cellar
in our chest
is that fungus
that's having fun just
thriving on being hidden
undisturbed
in the darkness
and the earth
fertilised by our shame.

The more we protect it
the safer it is
the more it grows
and the more we work to hide it
protect it.

Until it gets so big that it
overcomes us
and we are no longer ourselves.
Our mind controlled by a parasite
that hates the light
so builds a night
around it.

This makes it a vampire
we can't kill with fire
sticks
or bullets.
We must expose it.

It likes the dark?
Throw the spotlight on it.
It likes to hide?
Pull it out and display it.
It likes to be ignored?

Stare at it.
It likes the quiet?
Shout about it,
confront it.

Do that and watch it shrink.
I know we might think
we're not strong enough
but we've been pretty damn tough
to keep hiding that thing.
I know how bloody tiring
it is to keep pretending.
But we've been doing it this long
so clearly, we are strong.

Let's do the opposite
and we might begin to beat it.

Skylight

I own a piece of sky.
It's mine so I have framed it.
A plain wooden frame
is all it needs
its beauty speaks for itself.
I put glass inside the frame
to protect my piece of sky
to keep it from dust, fingerprints
and the sticky residue of time.

I placed fabric across the glass
to hide my strip of sky
at night
to preserve its modesty
when it drapes itself in nothing
but diamonds and pearls.
I like to think my sky
appreciates my thoughtfulness
as it rests from my enamoured eyes.

In the morning
when I pull the fabric aside
I see my sky as though for the first time
an unveiling, a grand opening.
In return for my good care
my consideration
my patch of sky rewards me
with a new picture every day.
Sometimes so bright
it throws a square of light
onto the floor
that travels around the room.

Now and then it drums a beat
on the glass.
On such nights
I lie
beneath my hidden piece of sky
listening to its tune.

I can almost feel its fingertips
tapping on my skin.

Book Review

When a book is ripped
dropped in the bath or
thrown away, its spine
broken
does its story flash before its pages?

I Met a Boy

I met a boy who doesn't own an iron
which is fine
because mine
doesn't do much
except gather dust
in a corner.
I met a boy who watches in wonder
at the beauty of dust sparkling
in a sun beam.
I met a boy who daydreams
and has nightmares.
A boy who cares
about those who are excluded, different.
I met a boy both wise and innocent
naïve and worldly
fragile and sturdy.
I met a boy with shoulders as wide as a valley
yet whose entire body
can shudder
even crumple
at the mere
graze of an ear.
A boy who can feel Earth's force
as though she speaks to him
her energy in his every limb
from fingers down to feet.
I met a boy made of earth and moss and peat.
A boy with roots in his palms that make them itch
and branches in his chest that make him twitch.
A boy who does the washing up.
A boy who lifts me up.
I met a boy who when I told him my deepest, darkest secret
shrugged and said he wanted all of me.

I met a boy who when I had a panic attack
in the middle of the first night we spent together
took care of me
did what he could
to help me relax and get to sleep.
I met a boy who hears what I say.
I met a boy who wants to stand naked in the heavy rain.
I met a boy who keeps in touch
a boy I like to touch.
I met a boy who knows the power of the full moon
a boy permanently caught in a tune.
I met a boy who has written me poems.

So now it is my turn.
I met this boy...
and if he plays this right
I might give him my heart
and my iron.

Why Do We Pray?

Why do we pray to a God
to save us from the misfortune
which, if he exists, he created?
Does a rat in the basement
legs broken in a trap
pray for man to come and release him?

God's Mum

If God had a Mum
she'd come along
and tell him to stop playing
such violent games
with his toys,
to stop making so much noise
tidy the mess he's made
and for Heaven's sake
stop torturing the poor things
in that ant farm.

Gun

There was a gun in my mouth
pointing down at my heart.
You made me think I couldn't love
so, I tried hard.
Playing a game
of love notes and mix tapes
pretending, trying it your way
desperately struggling to get it right
the way you expected it to be.

There was a gun in my mouth
pointing up at my brain.
I thought I was going insane
having lost all idea of my own thoughts
hijacked by yours.
My grey cells didn't actually matter
they might as well melt
till I was no longer there.
I was lost in your circus
whilst you turned down the lights.

There was a gun in my mouth
pointing to my cheeks.
You'd fired the bullet
and now the air escaping through
the holes
stopped
my words
from being
heard.

There is a gun in my mouth
that now faces out.
I've learned that
it wasn't me that was wrong
it was you.
And I'm going to tell you
my tongue on the trigger.

Mouthful

Do not speak
with your mouth full
especially if it is full
of ideas
and opinions.

Door

You are a door
made to be pushed and pulled
made to be cut
made to fit.

You are a door
you exist to be entered
you must open to man
if you refuse
he has the right to break in.

You are a door
you exist to be exited
by new life
whether you want to or not.

Don't fight the breaking and entering
the coming and going
there is no point
you are only a door
you will be left unhinged.

Idiot Check

Idiot check 1 or idiot check 2,
let's just check, which one are you?

Idiot check 1:
keys, phone, wallet.

Idiot check 2:
keys, phone, wallet,
lip gloss

and
do I know where I'm going?
how am I getting there?
who am I meeting?
will there be other people there?

eyeliner

have I texted a friend
the name of the person I'm meeting
the location, and how we met?

concealer

will I have to leave my drink unattended?
who do I call if it's going wrong?
what's my escape plan?

comb

do I have enough money on me?
do I have too much money on me?
do I have enough battery
in my phone?
how am I getting home?

mirror

if I have to walk
what's the best route
not necessarily the quickest?
will the path be lit?
is it likely to be crowded?
any dark alleys along the way?
underground car parks
woods
fields
subways?

tissues

what will I say if someone approaches me?
will the way I walk draw attention to me
or will my noisy shoes?
can I run in them?
what can I use as a weapon?
is my outfit too provocative?
is my sexuality too obvious?

is my hair too easy to grab?
how simple might it be to rip off my clothes?

tampons

if I am not walking home
am I absolutely sure of the best way home?
if I'm taking a taxi or car service
where do I go to hail it?
and how do I know they're legit?
if I'm taking the bus or train will it be crowded?
or do I risk being alone on it?

gum

who do I text
to say I'm back safe?
and who do I call
if I panic?

Keys, phone, wallet.

Idiot check 1 or idiot check 2,
let's just check, which one are you?

The Liberation of Women

Running water liberated women.
The washing machine liberated women.
The dishwasher liberated women.
The right to divorce liberated women.
The vacuum cleaner liberated women.
The right to an education liberated women.
The vote liberated women.
The pill liberated women.
Abortion liberated women.

Wouldn't it be swell if society liberated women
then maybe they could finally be free?

Gropadin™

Do you struggle to keep your hands to yourself?
Do you feel you have rights over people
due to your power and wealth?
Do you seem to unwittingly get yourself into trouble
but the cause of the problem leaves you befuddled?
You are not alone
and now thanks to a brand-new medical breakthrough
we have the solution for you!

"Doctor, doctor, I can't help groping women."

"Well Sir,
it's not your fault, you're clearly ill.
I shall prescribe you some Gropadin.

I think we'll go straight for the higher dose –
we can safely go up to 2ml at most –
but if you take it twice a day
it should help keep those pesky urges at bay."

"Doctor, doctor, Gropadin wasn't enough
I was with a female associate and my clothes fell off."

"There, there, don't beat yourself up
ignore that drama queen.
It's not you, it's a malfunction in your genes
so, I shall modify the medical protocol
and prescribe you some Gropadol.
It comes in a convenient spray
you can use it any time of the day.
Spray it once on your face
and twice on your sack
it'll make everything shrink and contract
there'll be no chance of committing a lewd act."

"Doctor, doctor, I still got in the buff
and told that actress to touch my shrunken stuff."

"Ah, I see you're one of those poor unfortunate men
I therefore recommend
that you always carry around a Gropipen.
If you ever feel tempted, even just a little bit
whip out the pen, engage the tip
and stab it into your bum.
Then in the time it takes to count from 3 to 1
you'll be rendered catatonic
saving you from any histrionics.

And if all of that fails
and there's a chance you might end up in jail
we'll just check you into one of our clinics
you'll see, they're great, terrific!"

Gropadin™ , **Gropadol**™ and the **Gropipen**™
are registered trademarks of
Dirty Old Men Incorporated.

Side effects to be noted may include:
a refusal to take any responsibility
or admission of culpability,
an increase in self centeredness and machismo
and an over-inflated ego,
an inability to see that a sense of entitlement
is the only reason for the patient's predicament.
Some users have reported impaired judgement
an addiction to out-of-court settlements
and a sense of perpetual denial
which may result in coma, death, or even worse, a public trial.

If you experience any of these side effects
cease use and talk to your physician.
(Of course, just as long as she isn't a woman).

What Makes a Man?

First, he needs to lift incredible weights
and he should always be the one that dominates.
He must be able to win any fight
and be able to have sex all night.
He'll count in the hundreds the number of his conquests
and have shitloads, or no hair upon his chest
(depending on the trend, his age, the decade).
He'll have the highest levels of testosterone
and do all the DIY within his home.
He'll need only one hand to swiftly unclasp a bra
and of course, be incredibly fast when driving a car.
A true man will be infallible at reading maps
and instinctively know how to wield a hammer and an axe.
He'll have perfect, rippling muscles
and have mad game and sick hustle, bro.
He'll drink the most pints when he's out on the piss
and spend all available hours in the office.
A six-figure salary is the minimum he makes
and naturally he never, ever makes mistakes.
In a crisis a real man always knows what to do,
whatever happens, he'll stop his feelings coming through
because the mark of a man is that he has no weakness.
And then of course there is the size of his penis.

OK, let's stop that a second
'cos that's some real-life bullshit right there I reckon.

Surely what matters is how he views other people
whether he's able to treat all as his equal.
His ability
to conduct himself with dignity
his capacity
for empathy.

The fact that he's patient, thoughtful, respectful
is kind and honest and gentle.
That he can take care of himself as well as others
he's prepared to speak up when it's him that suffers
can share his emotions when things get too stressful
surely those attributes are more fundamental
than any of those listed above;
a real man is not the one with a fist inside his glove.

It's the 21st century, it's no longer the Wild West
so how about we put John Wayne to rest
as well as Rambo, Bruce Lee and John McClane.
It really is time we stop putting our men
under such unbelievable pressure
it won't just help make women's lives better.
It'll improve all men's lives too
by ridding them of harmful ideals, impossible to live up to.

By trying to be a He-Man
he risks being a No-Man.
Men have a 4-year shorter lifespan
are over twice as likely to drink through the strife
and 4 times more likely to take their own life.
By trying to be strong they make themselves vulnerable
and sometimes the harm can be irrecoverable
when they're ashamed so suffer in silence
despite illness, depression, even domestic violence.

A man needs the freedom to be true to himself
to protect both his physical and mental health.
So, keep an eye out for the men all around you.
Show them they don't have to be hard
or be a lad to impress you.
And bear it in mind when you bring up your sons
because truly, girls are not the only ones

under pressure to be a certain way
men are having it tough
even dying, each day
because they don't feel that they can say,
"Help me, I'm not ok."

Caterpillars

Would you like to come round for dinner?
I'll make you a delicious salad
in which I'll hide a few caterpillars
in the hope you'll get butterflies
in your stomach.

Body Con

This is my bum.
It's not perfect but it's the only one
I've got
and to be honest, I really rather like it a lot.
It's useful for sitting.
It's useful for shi…
shorts wearing.

These are my thighs.
They may not be the Hello Magazine approved size
and they might only have a gap
when I stand like that
but they are steady
and ready
to carry me
to wherever I want to be.

This with the help of my knees, my calves, my feet
those too are pretty damn neat
they're scarred, sometimes bruised
often stubbly rather than smooth.
However, together
these legs have taken me on countless adventures.

This here in front
is my…
call it whatever you want.
It has a number of functions
beyond just sexual enjoyment.
I'm even told it can squeeze out a melon
although I'm not too sure why that would ever happen
and I definitely won't go experimenting.

Here is my belly
it isn't quite jelly
but it is a bit wobbly
and I certainly don't have chocolate bar abs.
I mean, are you mad?
Chocolate is yummy
belongs in, not on my tummy.
And that way it's super comfy
for the weary traveller wishing to rest their head
or for a cat or a dog to use as a bed.

These are my boobs.
They arrive in any place
just a fraction of a second before my face,
like army scouts
on the lookout
and ready to cushion the blow
from any foe
such as an invisible glass door
or if I ever fall flat on the floor.

My arms.
They have their own kind of charm.
There's a bicep in there somewhere
and a bit of bingo under there
but they can lift and hold
and hug you so you don't get cold.

My back is curved
my shoulders unevenly strong
my chin is double
my hair tends to be frizzy as well as long
my hips are wide
I have baggy eyes

I have wrinkles and pimples and dimples
and all of that is quite alright!
I will never be the shape
that the media paints
as the right one to be
and that is fine with me.

See, there is so much more to me
than just my physical appearance
and my body is not there for other people's judgement
or sexualisation
objectification.
My body exists purely to house me.
I can run.
I can dance.
I can pick up a cup and bring it to my lips
and I know that's something so very simple to do
but it's something that one day I may need help to.

I refuse to take it for granted.
I couldn't possibly be disenchanted.
Hey society, stop trying to make me hate it.
My body is the most precious thing I own
so, I'm going to love every piece and every bone.

Big Bang

We are moving
and I am getting smaller and smaller
shrinking towards a central point
and I don't know
if I can go any smaller
but I do
I contract further
till I am a speck in my centre
the skin is peeling off my skull
downwards like the skin of a banana
curling over and outwards
like the sweetest shavings of chocolate
rolling tighter and tighter
folding me further
then when it can get no tighter
I inhale deeper and deeper
till suddenly I am flung back out
bursting and expanding in a blaze of light
at a million miles an hour
exploding across the universe
faster than light speed
flesh shaking, bones arching
I'm still not breathing
further and further I go
yet I'm not suffocating
how long can this keep going
seemingly never ending
until finally I'm bigger than the universe
spread thin and covering everything.

I fall back dazed and seeing stars.

Two fingers and you turned me inside out.

Can Opening

Crc tssssss

The sound of a can opening.
Although I have my back to you, I know
it isn't coke.
Instantly it's like you poured the cold beer
right down my spine.
I glance at the time.

1pm.
Already?!
I shudder.

You no longer get hangovers.
Maybe that's why the ghost of your hangover
envelops me.
A stress headache hugs my skull
slight nausea lurches in
anxiety rears its head.

I know that from now it will be impossible for me
to relax.
I spend the next couple of hours in a never ending
internal debate
as to whether I should stay
or go.

I decide to stay.
I said I'd need to leave at 5.30 anyway.
By 4 you're onto the red wine
and I'm counting down the time
I have left to swallow my discomfort
and pretend all is OK.

We are not alone so I won't cause friction.
She's only young
but is cottoning on to your addiction.

Just before I leave you've got to the point
where you're doing that thing with your lips
looking at me that way you do
from beneath your eyelids
and I am so ready to go.

That evening I watch people share emotions
on a stage.
I hold back my tears.
But on the drive home
they spill
and I can't stop thinking about
whether I should stay
or whether I should go
from us.

When I get home,
tired from the feelings
tired from the crying
I pour myself a drink
to see whether it'll help me
like it helps you.

It doesn't.

Waterboard

My hands on your thin, thin body
so knotted and sinewy.
I slowly slide them up
musician with a cello
both hands a noose around your neck.
I give it a little twist.
Not too much
just enough.
Enough to feel it strain under my fingers
screw cap thread.
Then I quickly flip you
over
and force your head under the water.
Down. Down hard.
I use the weight of my torso
to keep you there
watching as your hair fans out
seaweed in a current
willow weeping on a lake.
I feel your resistance.
I remain calm
observe the bubbles rise, mix and froth
dark water below
white foam on top
like Guinness.
When everything falls still
I'll pull you back out
limp, soaked, surrendered

and I'll wipe the floor with you,
mop.

Outside

Chairs skip and roll across the grass
acrobatic gymnasts tumbling
their strong backs taut
celebrating a rarely afforded freedom of movement
their bare legs kicking to the clouds.
The windows whistle their appreciation
as the winking blinds mark the beat.
The table rocks and sways
to the very brink of tipping, yet
maintaining balance with poise
sequinned with raindrops shimmering
under the narrow spotlight of sun.
Socks, shirts and sheets swing around a tightrope
with no concern for the chasm below
drawing gasps from the applauding leaves
as the parasol ends the show with a cartwheel.

Why Reading in Public is Cool

There once was a young girl who loved to read.
In fact, more than love, it was a real need.
Reading in tents, on planes, or when eating her food
in the sun, in the rain, whatever her mood.

But one day whilst reading on the school bus
this other kid started causing a fuss.

Callous and careless they were laughing and teasing
poking fun at the girl for her passion for reading.
This meant that her feelings were thoroughly hurt
by the ignorant kid's disagreeable words.

But dear little lady, do please consider this
think of all of those places that you get to visit
there are oceans and skies, there are castles and houses
there are stables and clubs, there are windswept
lighthouses
there are planets and mountains and flowery meadows.

And think of all the people that you get to know:
the athlete, the pop star, the folk under the floor
the lion, the spider and those kids in the war
some wizards, a queen, superheroes that kick butts

whilst all that the other kid sees is the inside of a bus.

Words

Words slough from me like flakes of skin
floating away.
An airplane banner of cloud letters
disappearing in my wake.
Dandelion clock in the breeze
seeds scattered but never sown.

Then I heard you.
I went and got a net
so that when the butterflies take off
in the fritillary of my mind
I can catch them.

I got some thread
to weave their wings together
and make my own lyrical tapestries.

Birthday

I could do so little
but to you it meant so much
that you clung on
till my birthday.
I've never seen so much love
as I saw in your eyes
when I came to say goodbye.
Even though you couldn't speak
I heard it.

I heard it all.

The Dealer

Hey. Psst, hey!
You looking for a fix?
I've got some of the highest-grade shit.

Come, come over here!
Seriously, it's the finest gear
you'll find on the street.
It's pure, not cut, 100% neat.

I'll do you a deal.
I'll do it for cheap.

You look like a discerning customer
tell me, what is it you're after?

I've got the stuff that'll blow your mind -
the trippy, psychedelic kind.
It's called Allen Ginsberg.
You take it by the line
and I guarantee you
a bloody good time.

If you're bouncing off the walls
and you feel you need a downer,
or you're having some issues with your father
a touch of Sylvia Plath under the tongue
is the dose you're after.

If you're the kind of person
who likes to booze
a shot of Dylan Thomas
is what you might choose.
It'll be like there are words dancing in your ear!

Or perhaps you'd like a bit of Shakespeare?
You can swallow one sonnet for that warm loving feeling
or two for a bit of midsummer night dreaming
but don't take any more, the come down can be brutal.
I knew this young couple that were left suicidal.

And if you do feel like you're drowning
a huff of Stevie Smith will have you waving
and back to raving.

No, don't be such a cliché
I don't have any molly
but I do have some Hollie
McNish.
That'll make you see reality like it really is.
And chances are, you'll want to get naked.

If you want to dance to the beat
of a London street
try a bump of Kate Tempest.
Sure, it might make you feel sad or stressed
but I promise you will no longer feel repressed.

Over here I've got some Rupi Kaur
if something a bit more instant is what you're looking for.

Now this is some Oscar Wilde.
Does what it says on the tin, it's far from mild.
I even saw this chap once hallucinate
that he was in a handbag as a child.

For a similar effect
if you're planning a road trip
a dab of Chaucer inside your lip
and it'll be like you've got company -
you'll hear a load of voices talking funny.

Or for something just as effective
but a little bit cheaper
what I have here
is the open mic regular.
Now this is one that you can directly inject
and it's hardly likely to show up in a test.

So, what do you want for your next fix?
Don't worry with these you can pick and mix.

Basically, all of this
can take you on an unbelievable trip
with no sweating, no gurning
there might even be some learning.

Sure, it might make your brain swell
but that's from all the extra grey cells!

So, do you want to buy some poetry?
It might just make you see the world differently.

Photo: Mark Ford Chivers

Chloë Jacquet (rhymes with croquet, duvet and poetray) is a multi-slam winning, multicultural, multifaceted spoken word artist.

With a preference for straight talking and a penchant for rhymes and opinions, Chloë's poetry is both entertaining and meaningful. Her work deals with a wide variety of subjects, ranging from workplace discrimination and mental health, to the pressures placed on modern men, via her short term relationship with a biscuit.

A regular live performer at poetry gigs, festivals and literary events, her work has featured several times on the radio, including on the BBC. She has also been published in a variety of anthologies. She was 2017 Oxford Hammer & Tongue slam champion and reached the semi-finals of the National Slam Finals at the Royal Albert Hall in both 2018 and 2019.

Chloë can be found on social media platforms using the handle **ChloeJPoetry**.

Acknowledgements

As a child must write a thank you letter (see Mum & Dad you succeeded in bringing me up semi-correctly), so must I give thanks to a few people.

It feels fitting to start with my family - my mum, my dad, my sister and my nephew - who have always supported me, surrounded me, even though from afar, and been my greatest fans. Love you.

I would also like to extend huge thanks to Ben Williams for his belief in me, for always lifting me up, for his valuable feedback and for the incredible book cover. We make a great team.

Next, I would like to give a shout out to Tim King who offered me my first ever gig. It was pretty awful as I was so nervous I could barely breathe and I shook like a leaf the whole way through, but it got me started on this path and for that I will forever be grateful.

My second gig came from Clive Oseman and Nick Lovell. They both have been great supporters of my work from the moment we met and since then have become friends. They have always fervently stood up to my self-doubt. Thanks guys.

Extra special thanks must of course go to Josephine and Peter Lay of Black Eyes Publishing UK. We did it! This wouldn't have been possible without you. I can't thank you enough.

Finally, to anyone who's ever supported me, booked me, said something positive to me, thank you to you too, you've fed my soul.